FROM VALLEYS TO VICTORIES

B. LAMONT MONFORD, Sr.

To
Nichole
May God Bless You

Fairway Press
Lima, Ohio

FROM VALLEYS TO VICTORIES

FIRST EDITION
Copyright © 1995 by
B. LaMont Monford, Sr.

Library of Congress Catalog Card Number: 95-95189

Scripture quotations are from the *King James Version of the Bible*, in the public domain.

ISBN 0-7880-0647-9   PRINTED IN U.S.A.

To my wife Teresa, who has always been an illuminating part of my life.

ACKNOWLEDGEMENTS

I would like to first thank God, who is the source of my inspiration. I also owe a debt of gratitude to the Philippian Missionary Baptist Church family for allowing me to make real the visions God has given me. For their help with this book, I would like to thank the following: Tim Wolfrum, without whom this book would not have been possible; Regina and Janet, for taking the time to read; and a very special thanks to Mrs. Hildred Gwinn for motivating me to share my story.

FOREWORD

These are some troubling times. These are times that try men souls. Our communities are no longer a place of domestic tranquillity. Our homes are no longer the haven of peace, and the commitment that was once the base of family structure is being dismantled. Seeing this, one might raise the question, "Where do we go from here?" Our Christian values are under assault. "The academic communities can no longer teach "truth" without fear of being criticized, and everywhere you turn people are asking, "Is there no balm in Gilead?" No wise diagnostician would deny that our nation is sick, and we are afflicted with a virus called iniquity. This toxic organism is eroding our society. The author opens up two critical components for us to look at: (1) The family with it's religious and social values; (2) The society (community) with its secular and scurrilous virtues.

It is not often that individuals allow others to view them from the inside and close up, with all the pain and the shame, the hurt and the humiliation, and yet remain recognizable. LaMont introduces us to his family and allows us to live with and share in all of the religious, social and economic struggles, the joys and the sorrows that this family endures. Secondly, with all the calamities, there remains in him this strong desire to achieve, to reach for something better and attain certain goals, e.g. academic and spiritual. Like Paul, all through the book his central thought is: This one thing I do, forgetting those things which are behind and reach unto those things which are before, I press toward the mark for the prize of the high calling of God in Christ Jesus, and with that strong determination he moves us from tragedy to triumph.

Rarely does an individual place himself in front of a community to be x-rayed and walk among us. Yet this is what Lamont does. He takes us on a pilgrimage through the valleys of melancholy and then lifts us up to the mountain tops of ecstasy. There he says to each of us: we too can move from valleys to victory, if we would only remember that those who are led by Christ will never be denied by Christ.

Sylvester Walker
St. Luke Baptist Church
Dayton, Ohio

INTRODUCTION

I once made the statement during the height of my mother's drug problem that if anything ever happened to her, I would probably just die. Now it's 14 years after her murder on the streets of my hometown, and I'm still living. I'm doing God's will as the pastor of the church He used to nurture me through the dark days during and after the loss of the most important person in my life.

Following is my story, the story of a young man born and raised in Lima, Ohio, who saw many sad moments in his life due to the viciousness of drugs and the devil's attack on his family. His mother was a single parent who turned to drugs and prostitution before her tragic death in 1981. Even as the teenager became aware of the ugliness in society, the pressures that tear homes apart, he came to know the Lord at an early age with the expectation that God would bring his troubles to a state of peace. But even after trusting God, he found the problems became more unbearable. While he gravitated toward God in the aftermath of his mother's murder, his brother descended into drugs and crime. While he became an ordained minister and began serving his home congregation, his brother served time in jail.

But the grace of God has eased the pain, frustration and guilt of both men. The young man is still the pastor of his home church, while his brother is an associate pastor in the same congregation. They have turned their valleys into victories.

For me, this book is an opportunity to share the goodness

of God and His delivering power, how He brought me through tragedy and gave me the chance to help others through my ministry. I hope this book will show that God can turn a dreary midnight into a bright, sunshiny day. We can't give up in the storm; we have to hold on.

The reality is that we who seek to do the will of God, either aggressively or not so aggressively, will encounter obstacles. There will be days that we wonder whether the walk with God is worthwhile. If we live long enough, we're going to have some kind of struggle, a moment when we'll have to decide whether we will lean on God or abandon ship. For the person who is going through life smoothly, it is a foreboding reality that we as Christians are either leaving a storm, in a storm or heading into a storm. He who realizes the storm is coming is the one who prepares for it and can endure. Hopefully, my experience can help you prepare for your coming storm or help you cope with a storm that has just passed.

FOOTPRINTS

One night I had a dream -
I dreamed I was walking
along the beach with the Lord.
Across the sky
flashed scenes from my life.
For each scene
I noticed two sets
of footprints in the sand.
One belonged to me
and the other to the Lord.

When the last scene of my life flashed before me,
   I looked back at the footprints in the sand.
I noticed
   that many times along the path of my life
   there was only one set of footprints.
I also noticed
   that it happened at the very lowest
      and saddest times in my life.

This really bothered me,
   and I questioned the Lord about it:
"Lord, you said that once I decided to follow you,
   You would walk with me all the way.

But I have noticed
   that during the most troublesome times in my life
      THERE IS ONLY ONE SET OF FOOTPRINTS.

I don't understand
    why in times when I needed you most,
        you should leave me."

The Lord replied,
    "My precious, precious child,
I love you and I would never,
    never leave you during your times
        of trial and suffering.
When you saw
    only one set of footprints,
        it was then that
            I CARRIED YOU."

Author Unknown

CHAPTER ONE

RESPONSIBILITY

Saturday was G.I. Cleaning Day at our house on Hughes Street when I was growing up. My brother Bruce and I couldn't help lending a military name to my mother's command that we clean the house, from carpet to toilet bowl, before we turned on the television for our weekend staple of cartoons. It was our one duty in the household, and we performed it with pride and a tinge of reluctance. It was also my first, but by far not my last lesson in how to be a man.

Our mother raised us by herself from the time of our births until she died when I was 14. My father was deeply involved in our lives, but he and my mother were never married and he never lived with us. His absence caused financial problems, but, though we were on welfare, my mother took very good care of us. We had the best of clothes. If we went to the grocery store, we stocked up. And we had moral support. She was involved in our school activities. She wanted to make sure we understood that she expected us to be the best that we could be and that she would not settle for anything less. She instilled in us good values. Though my father married another, she never said a bad thing about him in front of us. We had to respect Dad, and we did so willingly because we knew he was a good father to us.

We would get privileges and we earned an allowance, but along with those privileges there were chores and responsibilities. Our mother provided us with gifts. She was our mother, so we were the beneficiaries of her love. But she also expected something in return, so we had to give. What could we give? We learned responsibility by doing our chores and acting like men.

As I look back today on those early days in our single-family household, I tie my relationship with my mother to my relationship with Jesus Christ. God gives us Jesus, and Jesus gives Himself to us. We receive the benefits of being a child of God, but we can't stop there. We've got some responsibilities.

I think too many times, people ignore the responsibility we inherit with the gift of God's perfect love. We are all too often caught up in the eschatological aspect of Christianity. We say, "One day I'm going to get my pie in the sky." But we very seldom look at the here and now. We look at Jesus as our Savior, but we need to recognize that He says in Matthew 16:24: "If any man will come after me, let him deny himself and take up his cross and follow me."

I think my grandfather understood the responsibility that goes along with love. He was not my biological grandfather, but he and my biological grandmother had been together since before I was born. Together, both of my grandparents played a special role in our lives. Bruce and I were more like their children. In fact, my grandfather made it his duty to take us to school every morning, even though our home and Whittier Elementary School were separated by only a small alley. It would have been much easier for us to walk through that alley than to have grandfather drive up Third Street onto Reese Street to drop us off. But he would not allow us to walk the short distance because he was protective of us, and we were his special children. Every morning, he would give us a dollar, even though we were on welfare and receiving free school lunches. Often, when he would drop us off at school, we would sneak back to Jimmy's Corner Store to buy some candy. Amazingly, when he found out we were going back to the store, he said, "You don't need to sneak," and he began stopping at the store on our way to school.

Because of examples like my grandfather's, I don't think we considered ourselves any less privileged than children who had both father and mother in the house. In fact, many of my friends on Hughes Street lived in single-family households when we were growing up. We had an extended family that reached beyond the walls of our house into the neighborhood. We felt like we didn't have neighbors; we had people who were just like aunts and uncles, people we had to respect. Was being a member of a single-family household a down moment in my life? No. In fact, it was what I thought was a normal life at the time.

But today, there is a stigma attached to single-family homes. That stigma was delivered to me as a young pastor the first time I dedicated a child born out of wedlock. It was disturbing to hear grumbling from some members of the congregation who objected to the dedication of a single-parent child. A child born to a single parent has no choice in the matter. The child comes. And even though the child is born out of wedlock, we should not withhold from God what God has given. In or out of wedlock, every child is a gift from God, and we have to look at that child as such. We have to love that child and do for that child the same way we would for a child that is born in wedlock. We need to take extra responsibility for the child that does not have and provide for him or her.

When I shared that with the congregation, I could see a sensitivity. Each time I have that kind of situation arise in my church, I explain to the young lady and to the congregation this is not the ideal way God intended for a child to be born. We don't glamorize it. We deal with the reality of it. The act that created the child was wrong but there's a blessing, and this young lady has brought this blessing to dedicate it back to God.

Many times we as a Church want to feed people spiritually, but we don't give them any Christian common sense, any "mother wit" as my grandmother would say. What we have to do is deal with the physical need; we have to deal with the social need; we have to deal with the ministry that specializes in prevention. Paul said in Romans 12:1-2: "I beseech you therefore, brethren, by the mercies of God, that ye present your bodies a living sacrifice, holy, acceptable unto God, which is your reasonable service. And be not conformed to this world: but be ye transformed by the renewing of your mind, that ye may prove what is that good, and acceptable, and perfect, will of God." The world will not agree with the things we are called to do as Christians. But as long as we specialize in pleasing God, then hopefully we can reach the world. I say to my congregation that we're called to be "gooder" than the world. Although the poor English may get in the way, what we're saying is that God didn't call us to be better than other people. He called us to do good, to be good, to live good, to love good. The only way we can be good, live good and love good is to present our bodies as a living sacrifice. Then, even when we do the best we can do in preventing the negative, we need to know how to adjust ourselves to any particular situation that has gone beyond the boundaries of prevention and entered into the realm of "I did it; I'm in it." Now, how do you intervene to make a difference?

Then Vice President Dan Quayle and feminist groups both missed this point during the controversial Murphy Brown debate during the 1992 presidential campaign. The vice president made the statement that our society has made it socially acceptable for women to say, "Okay, I'm a businesswoman, but now I want to have a child. I don't want to be married, but I want to have a child." I think that he was right — society had gotten to a point of accepting it. God's perfect will for the family is that man leaves his mother and father and cleaves to his wife, and the two shall become one and become fruitful and multiply. So when women's groups and certain liberal factions began to attack Quayle for making those statements, I thought it was unfair. But when I analyzed it more closely, I saw that both sides of the issue had gotten so caught up in the argument that one was totally at one extreme and the other was at another extreme. I took a different angle. While we're arguing about what is socially acceptable — though I don't agree that it should be socially acceptable for children to be born out of wedlock — what do you do after the fact? Sometimes it happens. Then, we need to work on intervening and instilling some values to prevent it from happening again. Yet, we need to deal effectively with what has happened already.

A perfect illustration can be found in Jesus's words to the adulterous woman who was about to be stoned by a bloodthirsty crowd. Before that angry crowd stood a woman who knew the law. The law says, "Thou shalt not commit adultery." Under the law, the penalty for adultery was death by stoning. When questioned by the authorities, Jesus challenged the crowd to show compassion for the sinner. As they look at this story, many people get caught up in Jesus's response, "Ye without sin, cast the first stone." We see the crowd dropping the stones and dispersing, each one going back to his or her own home. But we very seldom look at that which I believe is the most important message of the entire story. We see a wanton woman and a condemning crowd, but more importantly we see a compassionate Christ, one who looks beyond the fault of the woman and sees the need. Before He left, He said to her, "Go and sin no more." He looked beyond the fault and saw her need.

We as a society have to be aware that no matter what kind of programs we put into effect, no matter how carefully the parents teach their children, some children are going to step outside what the parents wish for them. What we have to do is be sensitive enough and compassionate enough that, after the mistake is made, we address that issue. We must instill in them the love of God to know that in spite of what they've done, we can make the best out of a bad situation. God is a God that responds to us as we are. He is a master manipulator. He manipulates the negative into a positive if we just hang in there. So when a child has a baby out of wedlock, that is a negative. But God can manipulate that in the long run to make it a positive. He works it to the good because God is going to be glorified.

The Church needs people who are willing to step in and take the role of a father when the father is not there and a mother when the mother is not there. As a Church, we have the responsibility to raise each child that is born into our community.

The African proverb says that it takes an entire village to raise one child. God becomes to us what we need Him to be. To a blind man, God becomes an eye. To a motherless person, He becomes a mother. I think God does that through the Church. God has chosen to do the works of divinity by way of the help of humanity. We as a Church need to be whatever it takes to win someone to Christ. Everyone in the Church has a role. Mothers know how it feels to be a mother to a child. It's one thing to love your child, but it's another to love someone else's child. I think God has called us to love someone else's child just as much as we love our own.

After my mother's death, the women of the church became my mothers. In fact, I have more mothers now than anyone I know. The church women looked at me as their responsibility. While they were saddened by the tragedy that transpired in my life, they didn't just have sympathy; they had compassion. They moved to the point of reaching out. I met a woman in Shiloh Church two weeks after my mother died. She looked exactly like my mother. I just stared and started crying. I thought my mind was playing tricks on me. She looked at me and said, "I know what you're thinking.

Everybody says I look like your mom." She instantly treated my brother and me as her own sons. To this day, our relationship is close. I still call her Mom. She did what God has called us to do. She became mother to the motherless.

In this way, we prevent the children of single-family households from using their situation as a crutch on which they can excuse the problems in their lives. We can't allow the children of single-family households to say, "I can't do; I can't do." We have to take the crutch away and offer ourselves to them. We also have to know how to say, "Listen, you just don't want to do." Richard Lucas, a professor of New Testament at American Baptist College, said that an excuse is nothing more than a lie, told for the truth and given as a reason. We need to differentiate between an excuse and a reason. If we take the reason away, all children can offer is an excuse. If they say, "I have no father," we need to be able to say: "But you have 20 fathers right here in the church." It is our responsibility, earned by the perfect love of God given freely to us from our own births, to be mother to the motherless and father to the fatherless.

CHAPTER TWO

TRAGEDY

I vividly remember a dream I had in October 1980, about four months before my mother was murdered. In the dream, I was standing at Mount Olive Baptist Church listening to Pastor Davenport preach a funeral service. Curious about who died, I looked inside the casket and saw clearly my mother's face. Up until that point in the dream, I couldn't see myself because I was looking through my own eyes. But at the end of the service, I caught a glimpse of my family marching out beside the casket. Then I saw myself. I was still very young, nearly the same age I was at the time of the dream. I believe God was preparing me, through that dream, for what was about to happen.

I started to see things go wrong with my mom years before that dream, when I was in fourth grade at Whittier Elementary School. I think it was a smooth-talking boyfriend, maybe 10 or 15 years older than Mom, who turned her on to prostitution, then to drugs. He had been around the block a few times and knew how to attract young women to that side of life. Though it wasn't anything dramatic, she would start to be away from the house at all hours. There were frequent visits by people we had never seen in our home. The aspect of those visits that Bruce and I couldn't understand was why some of my mom's friends would come over and go into the bathroom for an hour or more. We became suspicious, so we would go in and start investigating. One day we found a burnt spoon. Although we didn't yet understand what it meant, that baffling spoon was our first concrete clue that something was seriously wrong with Mom.

We would soon find even more haunting evidence of Mom's drug problem. Bruce, my mother and I had moved in with my grandmother on Central Avenue. Bruce and I used to fashion small basketball hoops by opening metal clothes hangers, rounding them off and fastening them to the top of the door. One day during one of our games, Bruce jumped and dunked the ball hard into the hoop. As he came down, his jarring motion caused a syringe to fall from the ledge above the door frame. As it hit the floor, reality slapped both of us. We had heard rumors of our mother's drug use. We had suspicions that she was using, but we had hope that those suspicions were not true. But when we found the syringe and saw her facial expression when she knew that we knew, it was like the whole world had changed instantly. The normal life we thought we had on Hughes Street became abnormal, not because of our single-parent family situation, but because of drugs. My brother and I cried.

I'll never forget the way we tore up that syringe and bent the needle before we returned it to the door frame. When Mom came home, she went straight upstairs and began looking frantically for the syringe. We took her to the door and asked her, "Is this what you're looking for?" I think she realized at that moment that she was sick. When she left home that day, she went down to an apartment complex in the next block with some of her friends. We followed her and saw one of the guys she was with shooting drugs into his arm. She looked over at us and refused to get high. She was hurt, but she was sick. You could see that she didn't want to do it, but she didn't know how to get off it.

Drugs and her hunger for them also got Mom into trouble with the police. She was once arrested on shoplifting charges.

She knew the judges were going to give her jail time, so she quickly left town. Ironically, the day she left was the day my fifth-grade class took a field trip to the Allen County Courthouse to learn about the justice system. After the court session ended, our class was allowed to ask questions of the judge. In front of the entire class, I asked what would happen to a person who was caught stealing and was supposed to come to court but left the city. Ironically, the judge, without realizing it, answered the question I was really asking: "It would depend on the degree of the crime," he said. "For something like shoplifting, we wouldn't bother to put on a manhunt." A great relief came over me, but I was also paranoid because I was afraid my friends knew what was going on with my mother.

Mom was serving a six-month jail sentence for theft when my grandmother died in 1979. They brought her to the funeral in handcuffs. But even though she was handcuffed and incarcerated, I felt a peace because she was so healthy and beautiful. Her eyes were clear and she looked like the mother I knew on Hughes Street. Though we were in a funeral situation and I grieved over the loss of my grandmother, I also felt joy because I thought the jail time had done something for us. It gave her one last chance to do right.

We moved to Vine Street in 1980, immediately after Mom was released from jail. At first, she was beautiful and healthy both mentally and physically. But her descent back into a life of drugs and prostitution was almost immediate. Not a month after her release, she went from being beautiful to where she had been before she went to jail. The late nights started; the same people began coming around again. She became defensive when we talked to her. Finally, we told her that if she didn't get it together, we were going to live with my father and stepmother. We could see Mother just going downhill, being sloppy about getting high.

It was no coincidence I accepted Jesus Christ that same

year at the age of 13. I think I needed Christ as deliverance from what I was going through. I remember people at church quoting Matthew 11:28, "Come unto me, all ye that labor and are heavy laden, and I will give you rest." I used to hear them sing, "I came to Jesus just as I was, weary, worried and sad/ I found in him a resting place and He has made me glad." I was looking for that, a peace I could have when no one else was around. Even when the storm was raging in my life, that is what I sought. What struck me most, though, was that even after coming to the Lord and being saved, my mother kept getting worse and worse and worse. I used to question God and say, "You know, someone told me that if I were to be saved and accept you, I wouldn't have to go through this. I wouldn't want for anything; I would relax." It seemed things were just the opposite. But even though I questioned Christ at times, I still loved Him and believed He loved me and would provide for me. I was 13, but I was thinking on the level of a 30 year old.

I was about to grow up even faster. Though she continued to take good care of us, the drugs were taking a heavy toll on my mother. Things were getting worse, and I began spending weekends with my father and stepmother. On Sunday, February 8, 1981, Bruce and I were on the phone with a couple of girls at about 3 a.m. trying to set up a date for the next weekend. My Aunt Cynthia broke into the call and said very calmly, "LaMont, Bruce, I want you to go with me. I'll be there to pick you up in 15 minutes." I hung up the phone, looked at Bruce and told him I knew something was wrong with Mom. When we got to Lima Memorial Hospital, the whole family was there and we all sat around a table by the gift shop. The doctors came several times to tell us they were doing all they could, but that she was cut pretty badly. The last time the doctor came, I slid my chair back from the table, all the way across the room because I couldn't stand to hear him talk. My mother was dead.

Instantly, I felt a hatred that probably could have killed many people. I didn't ask why she died; I asked who did it. None of our family members knew. That bothered us the most, but we continued to discuss the possibilities. We found out it was a white guy in a red car that could have been a Camaro. Recently a young man, who was nearby when the murder occurred, came to my church and told me he heard my mom saying, "Don't kill me, don't kill me." He said the man then took the knife and brought it down on her stomach.

My mother asked to borrow money from me on the day she died, and I said no. That was the first thing that haunted me after she died, and it was the first of many things surrounding her death that made me feel guilty. I turned her away that day because I knew that she was so far gone into her addiction that my money would only enable her to buy more drugs. It had gotten to the point in the final days that she was pawning my saxophone and her own jewelry to feed her habit when she was low on money. The day after she died, we were cleaning out the closet and noticed my saxophone was gone. We later found the pawn slip in one of her drawers.

I didn't want to be a part of her habit that day, but after she was killed I felt like I had let her down. Bruce and I had made a vow to take care of our mother. It was us against the world. But she left us anyway. Soon after, I confided in Bruce that maybe if I would have given Mom that money she wouldn't have been out doing what she was doing to get it. He responded firmly and reassured me: "You can't blame yourself because it probably would have happened anyway."

During those first torturous days after the murder, I felt guilty because everyone knew our business. The day it happened, the story was all over the television news. I can remember the anchorperson saying, "If you have any information concerning this homicide, please contact the number on your screen." They gave my mom's name and described how the police found her. That bothered me. I remember looking around at the crowded church during the funeral thinking that everyone was just being nosy. When I went back to school, everyone knew what had happened. My school friends kept badgering me, asking if I knew who might have done it. It was bad enough that they used to say things about Mom being a prostitute. Before, they really couldn't prove it; they had just heard rumors around the neighborhood. But now it was fact, public knowledge. I felt ashamed because it was something everybody knew, and I thought it would hang over my head for the rest of my life. I loved my mother, but I was ashamed of what she got caught up in.

My guilt showed up in my fighting, in my failing grades and in my attitude. My girlfriend, who now happens to be my wife, said I used to look very angry in school. People never knew what kind of person I was because I never talked. My guilt also caused me to be antagonistic to my new stepmother. I remember saying to her over and over, "You're not my Mom; you can't tell me what to do." And that attitude carried over to the household chores in our new home. Bruce and I would be asked to stay home and baby-sit our younger stepbrothers and stepsisters. We had to start accepting that responsibility immediately after Mom died. But we were used to it just being the three of us: Bruce, Mom and me. Soon after we started baby-sitting, I got angry and told my stepmother, "If my mom were alive, I wouldn't have to do this." I was angry and jealous of my stepbrothers and stepsisters. Why couldn't my mom and dad be together? If my mom and dad would have gotten together and stayed together, her murder wouldn't have happened. She would have been home taking care of us. But I never blamed my dad because I really believe he loved my mom. I think it was by her choice that it didn't work out. I used to wonder why.

I soon went from a decent student to an "F" student. I did just what it took to get by. It was killing me. It was to the point where I could be doing what some young people are doing today with violence and hatred. We didn't have guns then; we fought it out with our fists. That was the mentality of the time. But I was the kind of person that if guns were the thing, I would have been involved in that. It was a different type of anger then, though. It wasn't vicious. You fought with your hands, and you won or lost with your hands. I never was a drinker, never was a smoker, never got high, but I was a fighter. I would fight anybody. It was just something I had to do to get my anger out. I made up in my mind that I wasn't going to let anyone take advantage of me because I wasn't going to be a victim twice, first my mother then me. It's scary to think about it now, some of the things I was capable of. I recognize now it was the grace of God that kept me safe.

My brother wasn't so fortunate. At the age of 17, he had already begun to experiment with marijuana and to hang around with shady characters before Mom's murder. After her death, he immersed himself into that lifestyle. It was excruciating for me to watch him repeat the mistakes I saw my mother make.

My stepmother and father tried to keep Bruce away from the tribulations of the street. My stepmother had a rule in her house: Bruce and I had to go to church at least twice per month. She figured our twice-a-month visits to church would turn into three or four times per month. That worked for me. I started loving church. It was something that became a part of me. But my brother was rebellious. He only went to church because he had to go. Bruce would have to attend church on the third and fourth Sundays of every month because he had procrastinated the previous weeks. My bond came closer to Christ, and his bond came closer to his friends and his girlfriend. He was still getting high. Eventually, he left the house as soon as he was able.

He and I worked for the Powell Company and I noticed that every week — we got paid together — he was asking me for money. One day I asked my cousin, "What's going on with Bruce? Is he on drugs?" He said, "Bruce loves that stuff. He's madly in love with crack." Later, Bruce and I were riding in the car, and I looked at him and said, "Bruce, what are you doing? You mean to tell me that after all we've been through with Mom that you would go down the same road?" He couldn't say anything.

The whole sickeningly familiar pit of drugs became clear to me at another cousin's house some time ago. He was the cousin who, I believe, was the bad influence on all of the other cousins because everybody wanted to be like him. I didn't want to be like him; he didn't turn me on. One day, he, Bruce and some other cousins were in the kitchen, making cocaine. I watched them cook the drug, put it in a pipe and smoke it. They later put me out of the house; they would never let me do that stuff because they hoped I would stay clean. But I remember seeing the effect it had on them while they were doing it. Six or seven of my cousins, who all had the potential to do great things, were going down the drain in the kitchen with one another and a crack pipe in their mouths.

CHAPTER THREE

VALLEYS INTO VICTORIES

As our mother's death became a reality to us, Bruce and I began to feel somewhat responsible for what happened to Mom. We wanted to protect her. I felt we had failed because we didn't do enough to bring her back from what she was doing. Then I hated white people with a passion. When I returned to school after the funeral, a teacher at South Junior High School asked me if the police knew who might have done it. I told him that a white person did it and that white people get away with everything. I felt like that. All I knew was that my mom was killed by a white guy, and a white police officer couldn't find out who did it.

I was also angry at a system I perceived had failed to, or was unwilling to, find my mother's killer. About the same time, Betty Jane Mottinger, a white postmistress in nearby Elgin, Ohio, was killed during a robbery at the post office there. The local sheriff's department really didn't have any leads, but there was a massive manhunt that led to the arrest and conviction of a suspect. No witnesses. No leads. But they found him. I thought, "They can find the guy who killed the white woman, but they can't find the guy who killed the black woman, my mother." She was black; she was a drug addict; she was a prostitute. She was nothing to them. But to me she was my mother. What is trash to one is treasure to another.

I was numb. The only thing that relaxed me at the time of the funeral was bowling. The day after my mom died, I went bowling. I just kept asking family members for money to go to the lanes. I must have bowled $100 worth of games, listening to the pins fall, and it did something for me. Maybe I was taking out frustration, maybe it was like the more pins that fell, the more relief came.

There were two people, other than the support of my father and stepmother, that kept me from going over the edge. God put people in the right place at the right time. My sixth-grade teacher, Velma Green, was special because education for her was more than just getting into a book and learning what was there. She was the kind of person who would come into the classroom and say, "Shut the books, put the pencils down and pay attention. We're going to talk about life." She prepared us for reality and what it means to be an adult, not settling for less when you can have more. I often thought she was there just for me. I believe God put me in her classroom for my own development. Pat Dotson, the counselor at South Junior High School, was also very special to me. She was more than a counselor, and it was more than just a job for her. She would always say something encouraging and remind me that I could have a future. I hated white people, but I didn't hate her, even though she was white. Those two role models kept me from self-destructing at a time when it would have been easy for me to check out of life for awhile.

Even though I had plenty of support from family and friends and role models, I found myself fighting, literally, the demons that surrounded the loss of my mother. Bruce and I had moved into the Perry school district soon after my mother's death. Perry is a suburban district that incorporates a few blocks of the black section of Lima with the mostly white areas in the country. I was used to going to school with mostly black people through elementary school and junior high school, and the culture shock hit me. One day during lunch, a white guy said something about Mom. I don't even remember what it was. But without thinking, I jumped on him and smashed a food tray in his face. I fought until I couldn't fight anymore. I didn't feel bad about it at the time. I think I could have just kept fighting. What I was seeing in him was the man who killed Mom.

My life and walk with God just before, during and just after this period parallels the progression of the book of Psalms. When I first accepted Christ at the age of 13, I was in a state of naivete, or orientation, in which I thought my salvation guaranteed an easy life on earth. But my mother's murder subjugated me to disorientation, much like the psalm writer when he lamented his position and the prosperity of the wicked. There was redemption, however. It came in the praise and reorientation of being reunited with God after the trial.

In Psalm 1, what Bible scholars call the psalm of orientation, we see a naive comparison between the righteous and the wicked. The righteous stand; the wicked fall. The righteous bloom, and the wicked suffer. So many times when we as Christians give up and don't look for the way out of our trials, it is because we never expected a tragedy or a negative influence. We always think everything is going to be just fine. We won't want for anything. We won't have any struggles. Psalm 1 hints at that, looking through the eyes of naivete:

> *Blessed is the man that walketh not in the counsel of the ungodly, nor standeth in the way of sinners, nor sitteth in the seat of the scornful. But his delight is in the law of the Lord; and in his law doth he meditate day and night. And he shall be like a tree planted by the rivers of water, that bringeth forth his fruit in his season; his leaf also shall not wither; and whatsoever he doeth shall prosper. The ungodly are not so: but are like chaff which*

the wind driveth away. Therefore the ungodly
shall not stand in the judgment, nor sinners
in the congregation of the righteous. For the
Lord knoweth the way of the righteous; but
the way of the ungodly shall perish.

When I was a new Christian, I used to hear sermons that featured phrases like "Ask and it shall be given unto you," "Seek and ye shall find," "Knock and the door shall be opened." All that good stuff. I sought the Kingdom of Righteousness in hopes that my mother would be transformed.

After my mom's death, the reality of Psalm 73, the psalm of disorientation, immediately hit me. Righteous people do suffer. They do encounter hardship. Some of my friends never went to church, yet their mothers had good jobs; their fathers were home with them. They had the nicest clothes, the best cars. Their mothers were living while mine was dead. Here I am trying to be a Christian, trying to do the right thing. But I felt like I kept myself pure in vain. I doubted God. If He loved me, why would he let this happen to me?

In Psalm 73, darkness breeds light, and light breeds darkness. The roles are reversed:

Truly God is good to Israel, even to such as
are of a clean heart. But as for me, my feet
were almost gone; my steps had well nigh
slipped. For I was envious at the foolish, when
I saw the prosperity of the wicked.
For there are no bands in their death: but their
strength is firm. They are not in trouble as
other men; neither are they plagued like other
men. Therefore pride compasseth them about
as a chain; violence covereth them as a
garment. Their eyes stand out with fatness:
they have more than heart could wish. They

are corrupt, and speak wickedly concerning oppression: they speak loftily. They set their mouth against the heavens, and their tongue walketh through the earth. Therefore his people return hither: and waters of a full cup are wrung out to them. And they say, How doth God know? and is there knowledge in the most High? Behold, these are the ungodly, who prosper in the world; they increase in riches. Verily, I have cleansed my heart in vain, and washed my hands in innocency. For all the day long have I been plagued, and chastened every morning. If I say, I will speak thus; behold, I should offend against the generation of thy children. When I thought to know this, it was too painful for me. Until I went into the sanctuary of God, then understood I their end. Surely thou didst set them in slippery places: thou castedest them down into destruction. How are they brought into desolation, as in a moment! they are utterly consumed with terrors. As a dream when one awaketh, so, O Lord, when thou awakest, thou shalt despise their image. Thus my heart was grieved and I was pricked in my reins. So foolish was I, and ignorant; I was as a beast before thee. Nevertheless I am continually with thee: thou hast holden me by my right hand. Thou shalt guide me with thy counsel, and afterward receive me to glory. Whom have I in heaven but thee? and there is none upon earth that I desire beside thee. My flesh and my heart faileth: but God is the strength of my heart, and my portion for ever. For, lo, they that are far from thee shall perish:

thou hast destroyed all them that go awhoring
from thee. But it is good for me to draw near
to God: I have put my trust in the Lord God,
that I may declare all thy works.

When I was about 16, I re-entered the presence of God. I really started to see that he was there all the time, even when I thought He had abandoned me. I appreciated God more in the Psalm 73 situation than in the Psalm 1 situation. Now I had a real relationship with Him. I'll never forget standing at the kitchen sink washing dishes when I heard the voice of God say, "I allowed your mother's death to happen, but I'm going to make you a better person because of it." I do believe God allowed it to happen. He allows everything that happens to happen. But I do think I'm a better person than I would have been had it never happened. I could have gone off the deep end into the desert of destruction. But God turned the valley into a victory. So I took the bitterness and hatred and channeled all that negative energy into the positive. If my mother's death had never occurred, I don't think I would be as sensitive to the needs of others as I am now. I wouldn't be as sensitive to the plight of prostitutes. I wouldn't have a drug ministry in my church. I probably wouldn't have a serious youth ministry that helps teens with the problems they face.

Charles Stanley puts it this way: Whenever there is a tough circumstance in our lives, God is always faithful to give us a way out. What we have to do is be faithful and look for the way out. Then, when we find it, we have to take it. I've always looked for the way out. My way out was the ministry. Christ. The Church. The Word addicted me. The reality struck me that Christians do suffer. God's grace pulled me through even when consciously I wasn't trying to get through.

So, when I re-entered the Church, I realized God would get all the glory. All things really work together for the good because God is not going to let the devil get His glory. He'll take the murder of a young man's mother and still get glory out of it. Now when I entered the presence of God, I realized that even though there was somebody out there who killed my mom and got away with it, God made something happen out of it.

I can really praise God now, because of Psalm 150, the psalm of reorientation. It is like a trial by fire. I think it was a reinvigorating situation when I heard God's voice. I could praise His name even though there was tragedy. Even today, there are people I grew up with who don't go to church, who don't give God their time, who are seemingly doing much better than I am. But I know, ultimately, the righteous will be victorious, and the wicked will suffer.

> *Praise ye the Lord. Praise God in his sanctuary: praise him in the firmament of his power. Praise him for his mighty acts: praise him according to his excellent greatness. Praise him with the sound of the trumpet: praise him with the psaltery and harp. Praise him with the timbrel and dance: praise him with stringed instruments and organs. Praise him upon the loud cymbals: praise him upon the high sounding cymbals. Let every thing that hath breath praise the Lord. Praise ye the Lord.*

I don't want to sound like I'm wishing suffering on the wicked. I don't want anybody to stay in the darkness of evil. I wish everyone would come to the light of Jesus Christ. But there's a reality that some people are going to be left behind. We cannot let the seemingly prosperous lifestyle of the wicked hinder us from giving Him the best of us.

Another tragedy hit my family later in my life, and I was tested again. My stepsister was murdered, stabbed 17 times by her boyfriend. It was only the second funeral I officiated at my church. A woman who attended that service joined our church two years later. She said, "Pastor Monford, I joined your church because I saw you do something I thought I'd never see anyone be able to do. Here's your sister murdered, and everyone's crying. But you never shed a tear. You continued to urge us to trust God."

People wonder why I do what I do. It's because I'm a fool for God. I don't know how He does it, but He does it. If God can take that hatred and give me love in its place, if He can replace that negative energy and cause me to turn it into a positive, He can do anything.

CHAPTER FOUR

SHAME

I was sitting in math class one day in junior high when I was hit with the reality of something I already knew but didn't want to admit. My friends and classmates knew about my mother's lifestyle, and they were talking about it. That day in class, one of my classmates and I were arguing with each other, nothing too serious. But he said, "How can you say anything about anybody when your mother is a prostitute." I can remember wanting to crawl under the desk because I realized that what I was afraid for people to know, they already knew. My classmates had to know because their moms and dads and family members were talking about my mom. I became ashamed immediately. My mother was doing things that were causing my friends to talk about me. As a result of that shame, I was often held back from getting into discussions with classmates, even jokingly. I knew that at any time somebody could draw out my mother and use her against me. "Playing the dozens" is what we called the common school game in which two people say nasty things about each other to make others laugh. It's funny as long as you're on top. But when you're losing you pull out the heavy artillery. I've seen people say some vicious things to win the game. I didn't want to be the victim of that. I knew I would be if I played for too long.

When I moved to Perry High School the next year, I was around a lot of new people, people I didn't know. I always wondered what they were saying about my mother. I found out one day in the cafeteria. One of the young white guys and I were playing the dozens, and a third white guy interjected, "How can you say anything to him, when he could have had sex with your mother?" Fortunately, I was rooted enough in the Lord not to go crazy right away. I asked him calmly not to say that anymore and told him how sensitive I was to anything about my mother, who, by that time, had died. He said, "What if I do?" Then he said it again, and a big fight erupted. My past kept coming back. The reality was that my past would keep creeping up on me for several years. I decided to take matters into my own hands by relying on the Spirit of God and respond in the positive, not in the negative. I can't control what happened in the past, but I can control how I respond to it.

My wife is just now hearing for the first time some of the things that I've been sharing with other people. I was reluctant to share certain things with her because I didn't know how she would feel about being with someone like me. I don't know why I felt that way; I didn't really have a logical reason. She always loved me for who I was.

I was ashamed for what my mother was doing, but I was also ashamed because maybe there was something I could do to change the situation. I wondered if I had done all I could do, so I was ashamed. I think my shame derived from an assault by the devil. He seeks to scheme against us in any way he can. I was a new Christian, and I think that was the devil's way of trying to get to me. So many times we as Christians withhold valuable information because we feel like it will incriminate us. We plead the Fifth Amendment on certain things because we don't want our past or our weaknesses to be exposed. So we withhold them. Really, those weaknesses should be exposed because what we share with someone else can be a triumph to someone else and bring a victory to his or her life.

I think I felt shame until just last year. I shared it during our city's Study Circles program, in which black and white people got together to discuss racial differences and create understanding. It was an opportunity for me to set free some of the things that were holding me captive for so long. I was meeting new people and with new people there are always things you don't want them to know. If they knew from where I had come, maybe they wouldn't be as willing to accept me. When the Study Circles began, one of the pastors who knew my situation asked me to share with the entire group. The group was talking about the victims of violence. I was reluctant, but I did it. It was the first time I shared my story with total strangers. These people loved me in Christ, but they didn't love me for who I was. That's what made it different from the other times I had shared the story. For the first time in years I wept while I was telling them my story. After I finished, though, I felt such a freedom. It was all out now. I had no reason to feel ashamed in the first place. But the devil was the author of that shame. He sought to keep me in bondage by what I had done in the past. And even though I had not done anything in the past and the shame was based on my mother's action, it was still holding me back. I didn't really have the freedom to share with people. Now I'm free to share because it will help someone else. People come to me and say they are better for hearing my story.

Not long ago, I received a letter from a white man whose sister was killed by a black man. He was a Christian, but he was bitter. He had reservations when it came to loving, or relating or being with blacks because of that situation. Even though I have never met him, I could feel through his letter the hurt he had experienced. Here he was putting on a false face in his church when deep down he had feelings that were keeping him in bondage. And he was ashamed that he felt that way. But he read my story in the newspaper and felt that God had meant for him to learn from my example and be free.

God has caused me to be sensitive to the needs of people in the streets, to love those whom other people cannot love. I can do that because I've felt that shame. I'm not ashamed because my story is giving God the glory. I've been delivered from that past bondage. I know now that somebody's life will be saved because my mother died. The circle of life is that something has to die in order for something to live. Maybe it took my mother dying so that I could be sensitive to the needs of others and reach many people who could otherwise fall into the same trap.

CHAPTER FIVE

CALLED TO SERVE

After the experience in the kitchen when I heard God's voice, I realized that God had something special for me, a call in my life that would allow me to take the hurt that I felt and relate to the hurt of others. I knew even then, at the age of 16, that I could reach people who needed healing. I also knew that God wanted me young. He wanted me to totally surrender myself to Him early in life. But I wasn't ready at first. I remember trying to make a bargain with God because I had never been able to get drunk or go to bars. So I wanted God to let me go out for a year, experience the things adults experience. Even though I had never been a drinker, I was trying to bargain with God to do these things, things I wasn't doing before anyway. In hindsight, I can see that it was the devil trying to hinder me from giving myself to God right then. But my bargain was short-lived. The Lord said, "Absolutely not."

So many times we think, like I did back then, that people have to go out and experience the dark sides of life. But I don't think God wanted me to do that. In my current ministry, people will say, "Pastor, you're young. You've never really experienced certain things. You don't know what it feels like to be high on crack or to be in a bad relationship." But I think God has allowed me to establish myself as a pastor who is sensitive to the overall needs of the community. I always tell people that the best lessons I've ever learned were learned because I listened to other people. If my father tells me a bridge is out, I don't have to go over it to find out. I can take his word for it. The successes I've experienced have come greatly as a result of listening and paying attention to older people. We often hear experience is the best teacher, but wisdom also comes from people who have already been down the road you're about to travel. Some of the experiences from which I've benefited are not things I've encountered directly. I've taken the experience of others and capitalized on it in hopes that some of the mistakes they've made I won't have to make or that I can build on some of their successes. I saw all I needed to see in the lives of my family members and other people who have gone down as a result of drugs that I knew I didn't have to try it to know that I didn't want it.

The week after I offered God my "bargain," I got into a fight. It was a terrible fight. This other boy and I fought for about an hour. The crispness of the air that day made my chest feel like it was going to explode. When I got home, I knelt by the bed and told God, "I can't live this life anymore." I decided then that I would heed what God wanted me to do and preach his Word, starting immediately.

My ability to avoid the trap of curiosity was not because of any brilliance on my part but was a direct gift from God. Sometimes I look back and think that I didn't do things I easily could have done. There were times like around the kitchen with my cousins, when everyone else was part of the party and smoking crack, that they wouldn't let me be a part of it. Here are people who are doing damage to themselves, but they isolated me from it. Not only do I believe God dealt with me directly, but he dealt with me through other people who prevented me from doing those things.

Soon after God made it clear to me that I would neither stray from the right life nor His plan for me, I took my first concrete step into the ministry by going to visit my pastor, Rev. Frank

Taylor. Pastor Taylor commuted from Akron to Lima on Fridays and stayed the weekend. I knew I needed to see him and went that next Friday. I walked into the church during choir rehearsal, and all of a sudden everyone quit singing and looked at me. They said, "You look like you have a glow on you." I scoffed and asked them if I could see a mirror. But when I went into Pastor Taylor's office and told him that God was calling me, he immediately said, "I know. I was just waiting on you to come in." I knew then, without a doubt, I had my calling. It didn't take a lightning bolt or an audible voice from God to give me that unshakable desire to give my life to the Lord. So in the bargaining process, God won. He said, "I won't budge; I want you just as you are."

Pastor Taylor went on to relate to me the seriousness of preaching, the seriousness of total surrender to God. He told me that ministry is not a playful thing; it is a call to suffering. Many times the people you love the most and try to do the most for are the ones who respond the least. Those you try to help the most are the ones who don't appreciate it. I found that to be true. There's a pain that goes with preaching, but there's a joy and an addiction, like nothing else I could ever imagine. Though you suffer for those you love, you still love what you do.

Suffering wasn't new to me. I was now in the Psalm 150 phase of faith. Whatever happened, happened. Sunshine, *Hallelujah*! Rain, *Hallelujah*! That's because I had this belief that God would work everything out. The day I really recognized the seriousness of preaching was the day when I realized, while driving down the street, that what you say can bring life to people or bring death. A cold chill just shook me. There could be somebody sitting in that congregation contemplating suicide when you preach. If you get up there and play with people and make them feel good instead of filling them with the Word of God, you may lose them, and God may lose them, forever.

I remember going to a conference and Dr. E.V. Hill told a story about how he was going through turmoil with his church membership. He planned to go out one Sunday morning, curse the membership and resign. He sat in his study waiting for the service to begin and had gotten so preoccupied with the issue at hand, that he almost didn't hear a knock at the door. Finally, he answered it and there stood a man who said, "I just want you to know that I've been through a lot this week, and I'm thinking about committing suicide. One of your members told me to come here to hear you preach to-day. I just want you to know I'm waiting for the Word." The Rev. Hill went back in and prepared another sermon, and it was powerful. That same man responded and became an active member of the church. That just shows that you never know who's out there on the brink. You have to be serious about preaching.

And I was serious as I neared my first sermon at Philippian Missionary Baptist Church on June 24, 1984, at the age of 17. I spent the week before that first sermon in Gary, Indiana, at a National Baptist Congress with several adult members of the church. While there, I attended a class taught by Dr. Manuel L. Scott. The class was about evangelism and how to be all things to all people. I'll never forget sitting in that auditorium during that powerful instruction by Dr. Scott and realizing I really didn't have any idea what preaching was about. I thought preaching was getting up and doing something that tickled the ear, putting all the right words in the right place and making the people feel good. When I heard this man speaking on evangelism, I threw into the trash can the sermon I had been preparing. I was struck by his call for the Christian community to be sensitive to the cries of different segments of society. His charge was for us to be aware enough to "hear the lambs cry." The lambs are those who are hurting, hindered and helpless. The new sermon I prepared that week in the hotel room was entitled "Once I Was Blind But Now I See." It dealt with the blind man Jesus touched. The first time Jesus touched him, he said, "I see men as trees walking." But when Jesus touched him again, he said, "I see men as they are. I see clearly." The major point of the message was that so many of us, as Christians, have received the initial touch from Jesus, and we've stopped there. We've allowed ourselves to walk around not seeing things as they are. We say, "I'm saved, and that's enough." But God didn't only want us to be saved; He wanted us to see men as they are — hurting, helpless, needing our attention. The point was that we who have accepted Jesus have to get to know Him. To know Him is to love Him; to love Him is to follow Him; to follow Him is to grow. We can't be effective as Christians saved today but still in the same place next year. I had heard so many testimonials in which the Christian remembers when Jesus saved this person or that person. My question was always, "What has He done for you lately?"

The day for my sermon finally came, and the church was filled to capacity. There were so many people there. I think the community had adopted me. I had many aunts and uncles, moms and dads — people who just took a liking to me. They had sympathy and compassion, but, more than that, they wanted to be a part of my life. They came to show their love for me. When I walked out of the office to take the pulpit, I scanned the congregation and saw my paternal grandmother. She was so happy and proud to see me up there. But I didn't get caught up in that because I knew this was the beginning of a new life for me. I put my head down and prayed until it was time for me to preach. I was very nervous at first, but when I began to speak it was like God just lifted me. Everything I studied, he brought back to my remembrance. I began to share the thoughts God gave me. Then, I remember thinking, "Out of all the people in the world God could have chosen, He chose me."

Seventeen people gave their lives to Christ that day. I had never seen so many people come. Several of them were my friends, people who had backslid but came back and committed themselves to Christ. My joy was so overwhelming. After the service, at the height of that joy, a lady approached me. She stopped, took my hand and looked me in the eyes and said, "You stay the way you are, and God is going to bless you. Don't change and don't try to outrun God." She died a week later. That stuck in my mind because maybe God sent her there that day to encourage me as one of her last acts on earth.

After high school, I became the youth pastor at Philippian and went to work at the Powell Company, a local janitorial service. I had several jobs between my graduation from high school and my formal call to the ministry, and I think each of them prepared me for a certain aspect of my current ministry. For one year, I worked with a group called Fair Housing, trying to eliminate discrimination in housing. It showed me the prejudices that exist and the nature of people who would hurt other people. I also worked as a Section 8 assistant for the local Metropolitan Housing Authority. I saw that there were people who tried to make it but couldn't, even though they fought to get away from government support. It shaped my way of helping people. I don't just hand them what they need. I knew that I was called to give my whole life to the ministry, but those jobs prepared me.

Right out of high school, I attended Northwestern School of the Bible, which was a local, non-accredited school where the teachers were local pastors who had gone to seminary and wanted to give back to the community. I went nearly every Saturday for four years to be prepared for teaching. Though the Northwestern school offered a four-year course of study, I began to get restless after two years there. I asked Pastor

Taylor, my home church pastor, if he thought I was ready to go to the seminary. He said there were things I still needed to accomplish at home before I would be ready to become a pastor. So I stayed two more years and finished at Northwestern. Soon after graduation, my wife and I were attending a Bible conference in the South and were returning on Interstate 65 near Nashville, Tennessee, when I saw signs for American Baptist College. In what seemed like one motion, I exited the highway, went into the school, got an application and returned to the car. I told my wife, "I want to go to school." On our way back, we decided to do whatever we had to do, sell whatever we had to sell, so that I could go to school. I remember going back to tell Pastor Taylor. He was sitting in the same chair he sat in two years earlier. He told me again that I really didn't need to go to school. I responded, "Look, you told me 'No' two years ago. I listened, but I don't want to be here in another two years saying I wish I would have gone. I'm going." That was June 1989, and I was headed for school two months later.

On our way back from Nashville that first day, I told God, "I want to go to school, but I need to sell my house; I need to sell a car." My house sold in one week. Two weeks later, I sold my car. And people in the church and the community just gave me money. One man saw me in a grocery store and said, "I know you're getting ready to go to school. I'm proud of you." Then he gave me $100.

We rented an apartment in Nashville unseen. Thankfully, when we arrived, the apartment was fine. And my wife, who had worked at a K-Mart in Lima, found another K-Mart within jogging distance. They hired her with full benefits. It seemed like whenever we became low on funds, God always made a way. I came home to preach one Sunday. Before I got up to preach, a lady who has been like a mother to me had rallied the community and raised $1,100 for me. They didn't want me to go without. God rewarded my faithfulness. That's why I can't help but try to help other people. Wherever I am, it's because of God. I can't forget that.

CHAPTER SIX

OFF TO SCHOOL

Until a year before I went to Nashville, Tennessee, and American Baptist College, I had never been farther south than Cincinnati. Even after I told my family and friends about my decision to go to the seminary, I think people thought I was rooted in Lima and wouldn't leave, even for the purpose of personal growth. A lot of other people didn't believe I was going to do it because they thought it was a hasty decision. Some people didn't know I was serious until I was packing up and getting ready to go. I remember my dad was supportive, but I could see concern from him about whether this was really what I wanted to do. Some may not have wanted me to go. Others wondered if I could make it outside of Lima. I don't think people had any ill intent; it was more of a concern for me. But they had seen me preach and become very active in my home church. I gave as much to the church as an associate pastor could. I loved my church, my pastor and the people in the church who nurtured me. They felt like I belonged to them. Maybe they were concerned that I would never come back.

It was not that I was the type of person who made hasty decisions. This was something I didn't have to analyze, though. I felt it within my soul that God had called me. I wanted to learn more about ministry, to be trained to do more than just give a sermon and be able to know the wholistic function of ministry. When I went to school, I knew I belonged there. I felt like Abraham probably felt when he left all of his kindred and God said, "Go to a place that I'll show you." God didn't tell Abraham exactly where he was going but assured Abraham that he would know it when he found it.

I'll never forget the first day of orientation at American Baptist College. I saw and heard people articulating different things about the school. The student government president was there, and he was so articulate, his words so defined and his diction perfect. I leaned over to my wife and told her, "I've got a long way to go." Ironically, I was the one standing there greeting students one year later.

The first day of classes, I took a pre-entry test in an effort to "test out" of certain classes about which I already had a strong knowledge base. I thought I was prepared, but I didn't do as well as I would have liked. I went away thinking, " Man, I could have done better and gone on to more exciting classes." To make matters worse, H. Ross McLeron, who was the only white professor I had in the first semester, was my teacher in Old Testament Survey. I was thinking that I had come to a black college and here I was taking a class from a white professor. I didn't want to be there. But what really amazed me was that on the first day of classes, Professor McLeron gave an overview of what we were going to learn. I picked up more in that one day than in the four years before. It was like a light came on, and I said to myself, "This is why I came." It confirmed what I had been thinking the previous four years. I had taught Sunday school classes, but here in one day I had figured out how much I didn't know. Professor McLeron became my favorite professor.

On the other hand, I had another class, English Composition, in which I didn't do so well. After the third week, I was flunking. Even though I was hungering to do well, that English class was killing me. One day I sat down and decided, "No, I'm determined to do well in every class." Then I went back to the beginning of the book and began re-reading everything and redoing all the exercises. I felt I was going to flunk English at the time I made that commitment, but I was determined to avoid that. In the end, I went from nearly flunking to being one of only two people who received an A in the class. That blessed me. It made me feel comfortable in writing letters to people. It made me feel comfortable in preaching before congregations that I hadn't preached in front of. I was now able to speak and articulate my thoughts properly across ethnic boundaries.

In that first year, I learned that there are all kinds of people in the ministry. We had people from Chicago, California, Africa, the Bahamas. Many times I learned more in Griggs Hall, the dormitory, than in the classroom. Those who were seeking an education came together there and shared their strengths and weaknesses with each other. We all had a common goal in mind — to be effective in the ministry. Although some students didn't want to be pastors but wanted a ministry with the homeless or other specialized area of service, we all shared a hunger for sharing God's message with people.

One of our professors of Baptist doctrine, Dr. Charles Hudson, was one of my greatest inspirations. He was a retired Air Force lieutenant colonel and very strict. He didn't accept people coming late to class or missing class. He was more than a professor. I saw him once leave class and get a student out of bed to come and get the education for which he had come to American Baptist College. What was so unique about Dr. Hudson was that he had a bus that he called a mobile ministry. Here is a man with a doctorate degree from Vanderbilt University who finished second in his class, but his heart was for people who lived in the projects. He would literally go and set up a church in a project and stay there for a year or more. After he would get that ministry started, he would leave and set up a church somewhere else. He would go and get the drug dealers and the users, the prostitutes and people who were caught up in the darkness of life. That was his ministry, taking it to the streets where the people were. This man could have pastored a big-city church with a huge congregation. But his heart was for people who didn't really want to go to church, who were not really looking for Christ. Instead, he was taking Christ to them. He molded me to know that there are some people who are never going to come to your church. You have to go to their church. To them, that could be their homes, the stoops where they drink, the corners where they stand and make their money, the syringes that get them high. What you have to do is take them Christ. Dr Hudson did that. And his most effective witnesses were those who came out of the projects.

I ran for Student Government Association president at the end of my first year at American Baptist College. It was the first time in the history of the school that anyone had ever done that. I wanted to make a difference because the college was financially poor. I remember when I first came to the school, some new students were crying about the conditions. A brother named Monterey Lee said, "You know, let's not cry about the conditions. Let's make them what they ought to be." Even though I didn't live on campus, I wanted to help out with that. So when the SGA asked for candidates, I decided to run. Unfortunately, it was only two weeks before the election, and my opponent had been campaigning for the entire second semester. However, I won overwhelmingly by saying that I loved the school and wanted to make a difference. I didn't try to give long speeches; people see right through that kind of thing.

During the summer before I took office, I invested my own money and had some T-shirts printed up to sell. With the money we made, we bought basketball and volleyball equipment, among other things, and donated them to the school. Those were the kinds of things I wanted to do to show students that we can't complain about the condition of the school unless we do something to improve it.

I didn't share my story with my fellow students and professors at American Baptist College until my final year. I was preaching at Chapel when I did it. I told them they really didn't know me or where I came from. I started by saying, "You see me with determination to do well and get good grades," then went on to tell them my mother's story and the circumstances I endured to get to college. People sat there and wept because they never knew that about me. I had never shared the story to make people feel sorry for me; I shared and still share it to let people know that we can make the best of bad situations. It was the only time I told my story at school. The reason I told it so sparingly was because there are millions of people with stories to tell. There were hundreds of people at American Baptist College and other institutions who have sacrificed and overcome great odds to get where they are. I just believe when you are a Christian and are really in tune with what God's love means to all humanity, you can't try to take credit. I am just a fragile person in whom God has made Himself manifest.

During my second year of seminary, I finally found a church home in Nashville. I got up one Sunday and said, "Whatever church I see people going into today, that's the church I'm joining." I dropped my wife off at K-Mart, where she was working, and went down the road. I saw people getting out of their cars and filing into Lake Providence Baptist Church. I went in and sat through Sunday school. At the end of the class, Pastor H. Bruce Maxwell introduced himself and asked about me. He immediately invited me to become a part of the church as an associate minister. I felt like that was the place I needed to be right then and there. Although it was a large church, I felt welcome. The worship experience was illuminating and exhilirating, yet I still felt that small church situation. Even though the church already had several associate ministers, I was drawn to Pastor Maxwell because he appeared to be so organized. I wanted to be that organized so I could pastor a large congregation. I never did anything Pastor Maxwell didn't ask me to do. If he asked me to read scripture, I stood and read scripture, and that was it. Anything I wanted to do, I asked him first. He appreciated that, and I appreciated him.

I also learned that you have to love people. Even though Pastor Maxwell had a church large enough that he could stick his chest out, he was probably the most humble person I have ever seen. Every member meant something to him. It reminds me of Christ. Although Christ was surrounded by great multitudes, he was sensitive enough to feel the touch of a woman who needed to be healed. During the second academic year, I was on a mission to complete what I had started the prior year. I began taking 20 credit hours per semester. I wanted to work, but my wife said I shouldn't. She pledged to work me through school if I would work later while she went to school. I felt like I was absorbing things at school like a sponge. I was learning that no matter how much education you get, you can never become overly smart. I would laugh at the new students who came in and tried to teach the professors. Sometimes it's better to listen than to speak. I was in academic heaven, growing in the fact that I was leading leaders as SGA president. I learned that in leading people, you must earn respect, not demand it. You win more from people by loving them than trying to demand.

I got a surprise during that second year as well. My home church, Philippian Missionary Baptist Church, called me to serve as the pastor. It was January 1991, a full year before I would finish my final class in Nashville. I was scared and surprised to get the call. Our church had just gone through a terrible experience with my predecessor, who left under un-favorable circumstances. That pastor happened to be Pastor Taylor, my father in the ministry. So it was uncomfortable for me. But it had always been my hope to come back some day and pastor my home church. I thought it would be 20 or 30 years from then, after I had gotten my feet wet at another congregation. I didn't see the church coming open in time for me to come back. I stepped into the pulpit on January 14, 1991. I remember looking out into the congregation. It was almost empty. I asked God, "Are you sure you're sending me here?" During the altar prayer, I asked God to give me some men. My first sermon was about building on the firm foundation of Christ. I made it known then that it was my intention that wherever the church would go, it would go by building on the foundation of Christ. Nothing more, nothing less.

When I first went to school, I thought graduation day would be a day of relief. But when it actually arrived, I felt like it was just a beginning, that I had a lot more to learn. I wanted to get a master's degree and a doctoral degree. The questions we as students asked of each other during graduation weren't about what we were going to do but about where we would go for further education. We had to put some brick and mor-tar on it. There were experiences you could only learn in the real world. It's one thing to put it on paper and another when you've got people on the other side of your desk. I don't think I could pastor today as I do had I not gone to American Baptist College.

CHAPTER SEVEN

A DIFFERENT ROAD

Bruce Monford took a more circuitous path to Christ than his younger brother LaMont. Just seventeen years old when their mother was murdered, Bruce quickly immersed himself in drug abuse and crime. It wasn't until a spiritual turning point and a third stay in jail in 1992 that Bruce committed his life to Jesus Christ, found peace for himself and accepted the tragedy that occurred in his life. Bruce and LaMont now work together at Philippian Missionary Baptist Church, where Bruce is an associate pastor and runs his own addiction ministry, the Intensive Care Unit. This is Bruce's testimony.

My father is a level-headed person, always has been. My mom was a street-oriented person. LaMont and my father are just alike; both strive to do the right thing. But I was just like my mother, and I always wondered if I was going to follow the life she led and lose my life at an early age. Now there's a breakthrough. I believe that God gives life and takes it. And I believe that as long as I'm living a Christian life and do what I'm doing, that God is going to give me long life. The reason I believe that is because I'm trying to help people. It doesn't matter who you are, what color you are, or where you come from, I love you and it's my job to help you. I don't believe I'm following Mom's footsteps anymore. I was not going to live a long life because I did it all. Thank you, Jesus, for giving me this second chance, or this fourth or fifth chance.

When LaMont and I were growing up, my mom was going through a lot of different things: prostitution, drugs, you name it. But she, LaMont and I had a bond. We were a family. No matter what she did, she took care of us. She taught us how to be brothers, stick together, fight together, whatever was necessary. Up until the time of Mom's death, things were rocky, yet they were a bit smoother because we were all together. When she died, all I could think about was to take care of my brother. My family came from a background of living in the streets, of the fast life. That's all I knew. It wasn't right, but I thought it was right because I was around it all my life. I got caught up in drinking, smoking marijuana and on to bigger things like cocaine.

LaMont was never a person who drank or smoked or anything like that. He was a "square," as we used to call him. But he went on to live a Christian life. I had to experience some things myself. My mother's death can't justify it completely, but partly it can. It caused me to take a different outlook about a lot of things. I had never hated anyone, but I felt we were done wrong. I was very angry, angry to the point of knowing that one day I would retaliate and get revenge for my mother's death. I also got caught up in drug addiction. All I knew was to rob, steal and destroy. Every time I got in trouble, I blamed it on Mom's death. I held onto that for so long. It went on for 11 years, carrying around this bitterness in my heart. I would go to prison for drugs, get out and do good, then go back because of drugs. I didn't know another way to deal with it. I thought drugs were the answers to my problems. Once I got into drugs, I could push all the other stuff behind me. But all the time it was still lurking there, making the problems worse. I never wanted LaMont to do that because I wanted him to live a good, clean life. I was already caught up into the life. But LaMont was going to school, playing football, getting ready to go to college. I didn't want him to get caught up in that.

It wasn't just like Saul on the road to Damascus, but a blinding light turned my life around. It happened as my cousin and I were fleeing the police during the committing of a crime one night in 1992. We were going about 70 miles an hour when we hit a bank of railroad tracks. The car flipped over and I saw a very bright blare of light. I was under the influence of drugs at the time, but when I came down from that high and realized what happened, all I wanted to do was live better. I was really scared; I couldn't even function because of fear. After I went to the jailhouse the next day to turn myself in, a woman came to see me. She had never been to the jail before. She told me that God could open doors that appeared to be closed. Here I was in jail. My brother was the pastor of the fastest growing church in Lima, and he was on the verge of a nervous breakdown because of me. The devil was trying to steal my life at that point. But God's grace and mercy spared me. I was at the point where I had to make a choice: Would I live for God or live for the world? When I chose to live for God, that was when things started happening in my life. The blare of light was an eye-opener; it was the turning point in my life. I've awakened many times since then when a light is turned on, and I start crying. That blare of light scared me.

Through the whole ordeal, all I can remember was that blare of light, as if my life was passing before my eyes. I knew as I came out of the situation that I had to get a grip on things. When I went back to prison, I used it to my educational advantage. I got seriously into the Bible. The first thing I had to deal with was that anger inside of me. Once I got that out, I could deal with anything. When I did that, the Lord started working in my life to the point that I could forgive the person who killed my mother. I could honestly say to him that I love him. I want this person to stand up and for justice to take place — that's the only right thing — but I would never go out and try to get revenge.

When I was in prison that third time, I tried to get into myself. Prison is not bad for a lot of people. It can be an educational program for people to learn more about themselves and find out what it takes to live better. I went to minister at the W.O.R.T.H. Center in Allen County recently and talked to an individual who blessed me. This man, Bobby North, raised his hand after my talk and said, "Bruce, I thank the Lord for you. When I was in prison with you, you said what you were going to do and now you're doing it. That's hope for me. I know that if God can do it for you, he can do it for me." Prison was the only thing that was going to stop me from the life I was in. I didn't go to a lot of different programs because a lot of people went to them to have a good time or just to get out. I got into my Bible. I did a lot of praying, a lot of studying; I fasted. I did what was necessary to find out what I wanted to do. When I did that, God started working in my life. He saw the sincerity. You have to be sincere with God. And when you are sincere, He can move in your life. I am a living witness because He did it for me. I was caught up in drugs, in prison. Whatever you can think of that is bad, except taking a life or raping someone, I've done it. For God to take that out of my life and put me on a positive road, it's nothing but a miracle. God showed me what He would do for me if I would just put forth some effort.

I was a three-time loser. I had been to prison twice before my educational experience. The other two times, I would cry and call home all the time. This time I was at peace. I was ready to go home, but I was at peace. My prayer was that God would fix me up, then let me go home. Until He had made a change in my life, I didn't want to go home.

I'm not supposed to be here today. That night in 1992 wasn't the first time I've faced death. But God spared me.

Now, today, I can say, "Man, I'm happy." I don't have a lot of money. I'm struggling like the next person. But I'm happy to be on the right road. Instead of going to prison, I'm able to go into prisons and tell people about the Good News of God and tell them about how God delivered me from drugs. Now that I've made a change in my life, I believe that God can do wonders. I cannot take any glory from that. I made the choice to try to live better but it was God who took control. For 14 years I lived in hell. But now I'm free from that.

I'm not where I want to be with the Lord yet, but I'm getting there. I think I'm at a halfway point. I've come out of the gutter. Now every step I take forward God blesses. Even when I do wrong, I ask for forgiveness and believe He will do it. Before I left prison the last time, I told the Lord, "If I ever put another drug to my mouth, if I ever indulge in the street life again, I want you to take the breath out of my body." The Bible says you've got to fear God. And you have to be careful what you ask for because He will do that. And He has.

I knew I was at peace with my mother's death on Mother's Day 1995. The reason I say that is because every Mother's Day for 14 years was a day that nearly destroyed me. They were days that I could do nothing but think about Mom and cry. But Mother's Day of 1995 I was able to deal with it. I went to dinner and enjoyed it. For the first time in 14 years, I thought that if I stay on the Christian walk I'll get to see Mom again in Heaven. I believe she is in Heaven because she knew the Lord. I don't know what will happen next Mother's Day, but now I'm at peace.

LaMont went his way, and I went my way, but we kept that brotherly bond. LaMont used to chase me in and out of drug houses trying to get me to understand when a lot of people would have given up on me. Because of that bond, he continued to chase me. LaMont and I don't fight. Sometimes we have disagreements, but we forget about it. I'm one of his nine associate ministers. I try to do more than any of the other associate ministers. I don't wait for things to happen, I take care of it for him. We have the perfect brother relationship. We're on the same team now. He's not chasing me; I'm not chasing him. We're chasing the Lord.

The Intensive Care Unit in medicine means you're dealing with a very serious situation. In my Intensive Care Unit ministry, we get serious about people who are looking for a way out of addiction, any addiction. If there's a vice in your life, we try to deal with it in a support group point of view. It's a Christian-based program. We rely on Christ. I concentrate on drug addiction because my mom died from drugs, my uncle died from drugs, my grandmother died from drinking and my other uncle died from drinking. Pastor Monford can tell you anything you need to know about the Bible. He's good. Whenever I ask him a question about it, I believe he can tell me the truth because he studied it for 11 or 12 years. When you come to me, I can tell you about drugs. He can't do that. I stand up in front of 900 people and say, "Yes, I'm the one that used to mess with drugs. Now I've got a story to tell you." We started the ministry with six or eight people in December of 1994. By February 1995, we were serving more than 30 people. It helps me to keep on top of my addiction. When I see other people crying out for help because of drugs, it makes me want to help. This is my dream: One day I want to be a director of my own drug rehabilitation center. I believe God is going to give me that dream. I'm going to name it after my mom. All things are possible through Christ Jesus.

CHAPTER EIGHT

TRUST AND OBEY

*Trust in the Lord with all your heart, and do not
rely on your own insight. In all your ways acknowl-
edge him, and he will make straight your paths.*
                                                Proverbs 3: 5-6

I think my trust in God was more fully developed after I
paused, looked back and saw that God had brought me through
everything with my sanity and with a more genuine love for
people and for Him. I used to ask the question, "Where was
God when my mother was killed?" Then I heard that same
question posed to an older minister. The minister said, "My
response to your question is that God was in the same place
He was when he allowed His Son to be crucified on the cross."
I heard that as a teenager, but it came back to my memory
within the past few years. We wonder about things that are
beyond our comprehension and wonder whether God has
abandoned us. But when we really look at it, He was there all
the time. Being a Christian does not exempt us from hardship, but it does guarantee us that through it all we will ultimately attain victory. When you're growing up you hear all
these passages of scripture that tell you to trust in God, and
He'll do what you want Him to do —"Ask and it shall be
given." Many times you think that when you do that things
will turn out right. But you find out that just when you trust
Him most, things go wrong.

Now when I face an obstacle that has uncertainty in it, many times I'll be hesitant to proceed. But I've got the kind of trust in God that I believe there is nothing God can't do. I have the kind of faith that I know He will show up on time. It's not just for difficult days; He'll be there in good days as well as bad days. He's a God that is omnipresent — He's everywhere at the same time; omnipotent — He's got the power to do what needs to be done; and omniscient — He knows everything about me. He never changes. He's not wishy-washy.

It's not just a feeling I have. I am filled with Him. I'm in Him, and He is in me. I can see now how Jesus could trust Him in the Garden of Gethsemane, even though He said, "Father, if Thou art willing, remove this cup from me; nevertheless not my will, but thine, be done" (Luke 22:42). There are things that I wish I didn't have to endure. There are some moments when uncertainty almost gets the best of me. But now I take the posture of Jesus — "Not my will, but Thine be done." I let Him do the driving; He is the captain of my ship. Unfortunately, those are things people say a lot of times, but when things really happen, we make that detour and say, "Jesus, I'll catch you around the block. I'm not going that way." Sometimes I don't really like where He's leading me, but I've been through enough places I didn't like to know that once I got there I could look back and see it was a part of my Christian development.

Of course, temptation is always there. There are always moments where our trust in God wanes and wanders. The devil knows our weakest points. He knows how to whisper sweet nothings into our ears. But even though there are moments when he tries to get the best of me, my dependence on the Holy Spirit keeps me from yielding. As the Bible says, we have a High Priest who knows our every weakness. In every way that we've been tempted, Jesus has been tempted. Though God allows us to be tempted, there is always another way. Charles Stanley says that God is always faithful in providing a way around each of our temptation or trials. But we have to be faithful to look for the way out and take it.

I've not matured to the point where I'm beyond temptation, but I've grown to where I'm always looking for the way out now. For instance, there was a time recently when I was driving down the street looking to get into trouble. I was angry enough with someone that I wanted to pick a fight. On my way to the fight, I experienced a flat tire. In that way, God was providing a way out. I fixed the flat tire, but I was still angry. Then the Lord allowed a train to come onto the tracks in front of me, forcing me to stop. I had to pause by force and think about what I was doing. He provided a way out. Some people say that's coincidence; I think it's God trying to work it out. I look for the way out. I ask, "Lord, what should I do?" I hear Him say, "Go back home." After I see this is God trying to work it out, I have to take the opportunity. I've learned to trust Him enough that whatever needs to happen, He can and will take care of it.

Too often, we as Christians become too confident of our own ability. Christians set themselves up for what I call spiritual assassination when they think they have grown beyond temptation. They go out unprotected. I've learned that I need God in everything I do. I need His protection, His wisdom, His encouragement, His Word. It's like the President of the United States who gets so naive he doesn't realize that no matter how many people in the country love him, there are people who believe what they believe so much that they would kill him. A Christian who goes out without his or her armor on is worse than a President who goes out without the Secret Service.

The root of this problem is evident in how we become born again. Many people misuse the word "sanctification." They think it means Christians instantly are everything they need to be. I believe sanctification is a process of growth, just like the growth experienced by a newborn baby. At first, the parents have to do everything for the newborn. Then a baby can hold its own bottle. Later, the baby no longer needs the bottle; he or she can eat table food. It gradually happens. But there are certain points in the lives of babies and young children when growth is more noticeable than others. It's the same for born-again Christians. There are moments when you need extraordinary faith and there are moments when you just need simple faith. I've learned to trust God in the simple things. "I want a car, God, which one should I get?" "I want a home, what home should I buy?" I want children; I want to be a good husband to my wife. I have to trust God every day. Some people try to pull out their faith when it is a situation that is so big that they really have to focus to trust God. I have learned to trust Him in simple things. When the big things come I'm already in practice.

I couldn't put in a book a recipe or a defined ingredient which I could say would offer you the same thing God has done for me. I have learned that I can only do so much by myself. I will eventually fail. A lot of times pastors get into a God syndrome. We set ourselves up for failure by thinking we've arrived. It happens to lay Christians, too. We think there is no more need to pray or stay close to God; we're already there. But as a pastor, I've learned that I have to depend completely on God because of the burdens people place on a pastor's shoulders. Those burdens are far greater than we can handle on our own. There are programs right now in our church that God gave to me to do, and I had no idea how to do them. But when He told me to do them, and I stepped out on faith, He always sent someone to help out. Abraham had Lot. Moses had Aaron. When Moses went to the mountain and God told him to tell the Pharoah to let His people go, Moses told the Lord, "I can't do it; I have a speech impediment." God said, "You have a brother Aaron; send Aaron, he can do it." Aaron became Moses' voice. What I've learned is that God blesses me through other people. When I have a willingness to share the vision God has given me, I always have someone willing to come on and help.

When the Lord asked me to start the Intensive Care Unit ministry for addiction, I said, "Lord I really can't relate to these people as I want to. I can only go so far. There is going to be somebody who won't come because they would say that I haven't been through it." I suffered as a result of my mother's drug habit and my brother Bruce's cocaine addiction as a co-dependent family member. But no matter how much I suffered as a co-dependent, I had never been directly dependent on drugs. I could not know what it was like. That's when God sent me Bruce as the leader of the unit. Three years earlier, I would never have thought he would be effective in anything like that. Moses had Aaron; I have Bruce. I've learned to depend on other people.

I think the last four years of my life I've probably grown more than all the other years put together. It's about being a pastor and being the watchman over other people. I had to depend on God because I came to the realization that no matter how smart or how good I want to be, I'm not smart or good enough to lead God's people without God's guidance. Therefore, I have to trust God, and I do it willingly.

I don't know what the future holds, but I know who holds the future. I know He has my best interests at heart. Wherever He leads me, I will follow.

I know this: If God can replace a mother's love, He can do anything.

Now unto him that is able to keep you from falling, and to present you faultless before the presence of his glory with exceeding joy, To the only wise God our Saviour, be glory and majesty, dominion and power, both now and ever. Amen.

Jude 24-25